CRAZY-MAZEY HOUSES

SCOT RITCHIE

LITTLE HARE

www.littleharebooks.com

Little Hare Books
8/21 Mary Street, Surry Hills
NSW 2010 AUSTRALIA
www.littleharebooks.com

National Library of Australia
Cataloguing-in-Publication entry
Ritchie, Scot.
Crazy-mazey houses.

For primary school children.
ISBN 978 1 921049 84 2 (pbk).

1. Dwellings - Juvenile literature. 2. Maze puzzles -
Juvenile literature. I. Title.

643.1

Designed by Serious Business
Produced by Pica Digital
Printed in China by Phoenix Offset

5 4 3 2 1

CRAZY-MAZEY HOUSES

What if the planet got so crowded there weren't any normal houses left? We could end up living in some really unusual places!

Join Zac, Alice, Adam, Emily, Keisha, Rodrigo and Tuffy as they try living underwater, in a junk house, up a tree, on the moon and lots more crazy places. You're going to be very busy!

The Characters

Adam   Alice   Keisha   Emily

Zac   Rodrigo   Tuffy

Blue Mouse Maze

Follow and solve some amazing mazes! Start wherever you see a blue mouse. You'll find yourself going along some strange routes— have you ever travelled up a giraffe's tongue?

Hidden Object

Can you find the hidden object on every page? It could be anywhere—and there are lots of things that look alike, so be careful!

Secret Message

There is a hidden message in the book— can you discover it? In every house there is a clue to help you find a secret letter. When you have all thirteen letters, unscramble them to spell out the three-word secret message. Let's find the first letter together.

How many apples can you spot in the picture below?

(Answer: five, but check to make sure!)

There are twenty-six letters in the alphabet; what is the fifth letter of the alphabet?

(Answer: E)

Now you have your first letter. Good luck finding the rest!

Don't forget...

At the back of the book you'll find fascinating facts about the crazy houses you've just seen. (Don't look now, but that's where the answers are as well.)

Happy House Hunting!

Junk House

There is plenty to do in this junk house.
And somebody else wants to join in.
Keisha has spotted a bear trying to get
into the kitchen—let's help her get over
there and scare him off!

Secret Letter Clue:

How many cats can you find?

Can you spot this toaster?

Underwater House

This underwater house is soaking wet. And it's veering off course! Zac has to boot the octopus off the computer or they could crash. Let's help him get there.

Secret Letter Clue:

How many octopuses can you find?

Can you spot this coffeepot?

Rooftop House

Most buildings have a roof, so why not live up there? Everyone looks right at home, but Tuffy has spotted a leak in the water tower. Let's get over there and help him fix it.

Secret Letter clue:

How many flags can you find?

Can you spot this candle?

Cave House

Adam has discovered one problem with living in a cave. Something is blocking the hole in the roof and the smoke can't escape. Can you help him find his way up there?

Secret Letter Clue:

How many bats can you find?

Can you spot this brush?

Desert House

Tuffy has found the only water in the whole desert—and it looks like he's in trouble! Alice is on her way to rescue him but she could use some help. Look out for rattlesnakes on the way.

Secret Letter Clue:

How many geckos can you find?

Can you spot this butterfly net?

Moon House

It looks like they'll have to share this house. The housemates seem nice enough, but maybe they are a bit too curious. Keisha looks worried. Let's help Emily rescue her!

Secret Letter Clue:

How many pillows can you find?

Can you spot this blaster gun?

CLoud House

Who is that getting thrown around by the tornado? It looks like Zac! Luckily Rodrigo and Keisha have found some jet packs, so help is on the way. Can you show them a route through the clouds?

SecreT LeTTer cLue:

How many angels can you find?

Can you spot this umbrella?

Alien House

It's a long way to this planet where the aliens live. Adam has dropped the multi-coloured Time Transformer, and without it they'll be stuck here forever. It's going to be hard to find! Can you help him?

Secret Letter clue:

How many aliens can you find?

Can you spot this alien hat?

Tree House

Tuffy is in trouble again. He's stuck on the roof of the shed, up a tree! It looks like we might have to travel through a giraffe to get to him. Hold your breath!

Secret Letter Clue:

How many monkeys can you find?

Can you spot this saw?

Bridge House

Zac has seen an orange support wire coming undone on this bridge house. If it unravels the whole house will come crashing down! Can you see which one? Let's go and fix it.

Secret Letter Clue:

How many seagulls can you find?

Can you spot this screwdriver?

JUNK HOUSE

Eventually everything turns into garbage. But a lot of what we throw away still has years of use left in it. With a bit of cleaning up and repair many things can be brought back to life. Tyres from trucks and cars are a good example—they can have a second life as insulation or even furniture.

UNDERWATER HOUSE

People live on one third of the earth's surface—the land. The other two-thirds is covered by water. French explorer Jacques Cousteau was convinced that we could one day install gills on our necks and live under the sea. Now we have an invention which allows us to breathe just like fish—by using air that dissolves in water.

ROOFTOP HOUSE

Living on a rooftop is not such a crazy idea. Turf rooftops have been used for centuries. Now technology allows people to plant more than ever on roofs. These 'green roofs' are good for the environment and help cool down buildings by insulating the building from the sun. And you can play ball on them too!

CAVE HOUSE

Do you want to live in a cave? Well, you can if you move to Spain. These modern cave dwellers have running water and electricity. In many ways caves are the safest and most ecologically friendly place to live. They are quiet and maintain a steady temperature because of the insulation of the earth.

DESERT HOUSE

Deserts cover 22 million square kilometres of the earth's surface. They are hot and dry and most have very little water. Animals who live there have adapted so they can get enough water from what they eat. People can live in deserts, too, but they need at least some water to survive.

MOON HOUSE

One advantage to living on the moon is that it is relatively close by (only 400,000 kilometres away!). A disadvantage is that the moon has almost no atmosphere, so we would have to create our own. Also the low gravity, although fun for jumping, would eventually cause our limbs to grow weak and to shrink.

MAN-MADE ISLAND HOUSE

Imagine houses constructed at sea like a giant puzzle. Houses pre-made in a factory for man-made islands are a good idea for an overcrowded planet. They are cheap and don't take up valuable land. In Holland people have been taking land back from the sea for centuries, and now they are trying out floating houses.

CLOUD HOUSE

Some scientists who study clouds believe that the only things that can survive up there are bacteria—and only for a while because the kind of clouds that could carry them only last half an hour. That's hardly time to set up house! Clouds are made up of billions of water droplets, so we'd be wet a lot of the time.

DRAIN HOUSE

Every city has a system of sewers and pipes running underneath it. As a place to live, a drain may not seem very attractive at first, but they do provide a lot of what we look for in a home— shelter, warmth, running water and plenty of space. And it would be a great place to keep your pet alligator.

ALIEN HOUSE

So far, the earth is the only place we know where life exists. But scientists know that some meteorites carry sugars and amino acids—the basis for living cells. Every year tonnes of meteorites crash onto the various planets, so who knows whether these 'space seeds' have taken root anywhere else.

TREE HOUSE

Many kinds of birds, snakes, mammals and insects already live in trees. These animals are built for life above the ground, but humans would have to make structures to live in. The good thing about trees is that we can always plant more, but it could take fifty years for them to grow large enough for us to build homes in.

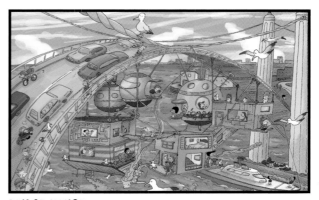

BRIDGE HOUSE

Apart from trolls and swallows, not much lives under bridges. But in an overcrowded world bridges could be a great location for a home. The road above provides a solid roof, and bridges are usually close to transport and water. For city dwellers that's a dream come true—a short commute!

SoLuTioNs

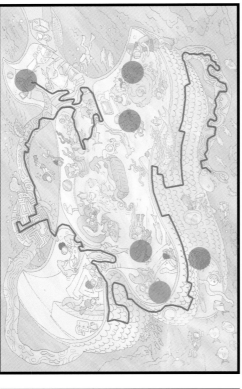

UNDERWATER HOUSE
Answer: 5 octopuses (letter E)

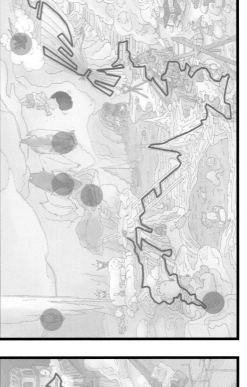

CAVE HOUSE
Answer: 5 bats (letter E)

JUNK HOUSE
Answer: 20 cats (letter T)

ROOFTOP HOUSE
Answer: 19 flags (letter S)